Cambridge English Readers

Level 4

Series editor: Philip Prowse

The Fruitcake Special and other stories

Frank Brennan

CAMBRIDGE
UNIVERSITY PRESS

CAMBRIDGE UNIVERSITY PRESS
Cambridge, New York, Melbourne, Madrid, Cape Town, Singapore, São Paulo

Cambridge University Press
The Edinburgh Building, Cambridge CB2 2RU, UK

www.cambridge.org
Information on this title: www.cambridge.org/9780521783651

First published 2000
9th printing 2005

Printed in India by Thomson Press

A catalogue record for this publication is available from the British Library

ISBN-13 978-0-521-78365-1 paperback
ISBN-10 0-521-78365-8 paperback

ISBN-13 978-0-521-78366-8 cassette
ISBN-10 0-521-78366-6 cassette

Contents

The Fruitcake Special

I never thought I would discover something quite so amazing by accident. I was a chemist at the Amos Cosmetics factory in New Jersey, USA, trying to design a new perfume when it happened.

I was trying out all the usual mix of flowers and things – just like I always did – when I decided to throw in a piece of the fruitcake Momma had packed for my lunch. I don't know why I did it – I just did.

I put it into the mix with all the other things. Before long, I had a little bottle of perfume made from the things I had mixed together. I put some on the back of my hand. I thought it smelled nice, but there was nothing special about it, so I put the bottle into my handbag. I couldn't give something like that to my boss. After all, I am a chemist and my job is to make perfumes in a proper way. If I told him how I made this one he would tell me not to be a silly girl. Later, he would probably make a joke about it to his friends at the golf club.

That's the kind of man my boss was.

'Anna!'

It was my boss, David Amos, the owner of Amos Cosmetics. He happened to be walking past where I worked. He never usually spoke to people like me. What did he want? I felt nervous.

'Yes, Mr Amos,' I said.

'You're looking terrific today! Mmm . . . what's that lovely smell? It's like fresh bread and flowers and sunshine all mixed together with . . . I don't know – is it you, Anna?'

I didn't know what he was talking about. I couldn't smell anything special.

Mr Amos had an expert nose for perfumes. And he knew it.

'Yes, it is you!' he said loudly. All the other chemists nearby could hear. It was embarrassing.

I had never heard my boss speak to me like that before. Or to anybody else, come to think of it. David Amos is a dark, handsome English guy who would never dream of saying nice things to ordinary looking girls like me. He preferred to be with pretty young models who liked his appearance and his money. When he did speak to the chemists he was usually complaining about something. Was he playing some kind of joke today?

Suddenly he came over right next to me. He spoke in a quiet voice close to my ear.

'You know, Anna, I've never really noticed it before – I can't think why – but you really are a beautiful woman!'

'Mr Amos. I . . .' I tried to answer but I didn't know what to say.

'No, it's true, Anna,' he said. 'I must see you outside this dull factory. Will you have dinner with me tonight?'

'Well, I . . .' I was still too surprised to speak properly.

'That's great! I'll pick you up at your place tonight at eight. See you then,' he said.

He was gone before I could say anything.

As I went home on the bus I thought of the strange situation I was in. My boss, who was famous for going out with beautiful women, had told me I was beautiful and had asked me out! But I know I am just ordinary looking and not his usual type at all. When I got home my Momma was in the sitting room talking to my Aunt Mimi.

Aunt Mimi. I like my Aunt Mimi, but she simply can't mind her own business. She has wanted me to find a husband for ages. She didn't like the thought of me being single and having a career. She thought it wasn't natural for a twenty-seven-year-old woman like me not to be married. Aunt Mimi thought that the least she could do for me was to find me a husband. I was used to this by now, but it was still embarrassing.

'Aunt Mimi – how nice to see you,' I said.

Aunt Mimi looked at me and smiled. 'Anna, my little girl . . . but look at you: you're not a little girl any more, you're a twenty-three-year-old woman already! How time flies!'

'Actually, I'm twenty-seven, Aunt Mimi,' I said. She always got my age wrong.

'So soon? And you're not married yet? Your mother was married when she was eighteen. Eighteen! And you were born when she was nineteen!' Aunt Mimi looked sad as she said this.

She decided to say what she thought at once – as she always did.

'So when are you going bring a nice boy home?' she asked, looking me right in the eye.

'There was that boy Armstrong you saw two years ago. He was nice,' said Momma, trying to help me.

'Momma, Armstrong was the pizza delivery man,' I tried to explain, but Momma never did listen.

'Armstrong was here a few times. I liked him,' said Momma.

'Momma,' I said, 'that was when the cooker broke down – remember? We ate pizzas for almost a week until it was fixed. Armstrong just delivered the pizzas.'

'I don't care,' said Momma. 'I liked him – he had nice eyes.'

Aunt Mimi raised her eyes in surprise.

'You mean to say you let this Armstrong boy go?' said Aunt Mimi.

'But he was only the pizza delivery man,' I said, weakly.

'Then he was. By now he probably owns the company!' said Aunt Mimi. 'And you let him go! Anna!'

It was no use arguing. I knew they were not going to listen to me. So I changed the subject.

'That fruitcake was nice, Momma,' I said.

'Aunt Mimi brought it,' said Momma. 'But don't change the subject – your aunt has something to say to you.'

Oh no! She's trying to find a husband for me again!

Aunt Mimi began, 'I've found the perfect boy for you, Anna. Well . . . he's not exactly young, but neither are you any more . . . and he's still got his own hair . . .'

I decided I had to put a stop to this – I didn't want to meet Aunt Mimi's 'boy' even if he did have his own hair.

'Thanks, Aunt Mimi,' I said. 'But I'm already seeing someone tonight.'

I hadn't meant to tell them but I had to do something to stop Aunt Mimi. It certainly surprised them. They both looked at me with their eyes and mouths wide open like a couple of fish.

'Yes,' I went on. 'I'm going out with my boss, Mr Amos. He's picking me up at eight.'

That certainly surprised them!

* * *

Momma and Aunt Mimi were very pleased, of course. They went off together to plan the wedding and left me to get ready for the man they hoped would be my future husband. I was beginning to wish I hadn't told them. After all, I had no idea why my boss had behaved towards me in that way. He had never even noticed me before now. However, he had noticed the perfume I had been wearing. Lately I had been wearing a perfume called *Intrigue*. It was made by another company and I actually preferred it to the perfumes we made. Mr Amos did have a very good nose for perfumes. Perhaps *Intrigue* was so good he just couldn't stop himself. Who knows?

Anyway, I had to get ready for my evening out. Although I couldn't explain why Mr Amos had suddenly found me attractive, I really wanted to find out. In my own way I'm as bad as my Aunt Mimi, I guess. The funny thing was, I don't really like men like Mr Amos. But I wanted to find out why he had changed.

So I put on my best black dress, lots and lots of *Intrigue* and my one pair of high-heeled shoes. The handbag I use for work is the only one I've got because I don't go out that often. I took it. Then I heard the doorbell ring.

Momma and Aunt Mimi were at the front door before I could move. They wanted to see my date. Both of them were trying to get me to hurry up. They had big smiles on their faces.

I opened the door.

'Hello, Anna.'

It was Mr Amos. He looked very handsome. However, he was quieter than before and was looking down at the floor. I could hear Momma and Aunt Mimi behind me. I could tell they liked him. It was embarrassing.

'Hello, Mr Amos,' I said.

I was expecting him to say something friendly, like 'Call me David' or something. But he didn't.

I managed to get him away from my Momma and Aunt Mimi without too much trouble. I guess they thought we should be alone together if they had any hope of hearing wedding bells in the future.

He hardly said anything in his car, either, apart from polite conversation about how nice I looked. I could tell he didn't mean it. Men have a way of calling you 'nice' when they really mean they don't care how you look.

Anyway, he drove me to an expensive French restaurant where we spent some time having drinks and ordering food. All the conversation was of the polite kind, but I could tell he was getting ready to say something. Then he turned to me with a serious look on his face and spoke.

'Look Anna . . .' he began.

I knew it! He'd changed his mind and was trying to think of some excuse to get out of our evening together.

'. . . about today, at the factory,' he continued. 'I don't know why I behaved like that.'

'I thought it was because you found me attractive, Mr Amos. And because you liked my perfume,' I said, wondering why the *Intrigue* I was wearing didn't seem to be having any effect on him. But it was obvious he hadn't been listening to me.

'You see, Anna,' he said, 'if we can see this as . . . as . . .'

'As what, Mr Amos?' I asked.

He suddenly put on a smile. 'As a reward for all your hard work at the factory. After all, you are one of our best chemists. It's the least I can do to show how much I value your efforts. Have this meal on me! I'll pay for it!'

If the meal had been there it would really have been on him – I would have thrown it at him! So he had changed his mind and now wanted to get rid of me. I didn't believe for one moment that this meal was a prize for being a good little chemist. I needed to be on my own to think what to do.

'Excuse me for a moment, Mr Amos,' I said, getting up from my seat.

'Of course,' he answered, looking less nervous than before.

I went to the ladies' room. I felt like breaking the furniture or something. I was annoyed! I had my pride, after all! And why hadn't my *Intrigue* worked? Perhaps I hadn't put enough on, even for his expert nose. I decided to put a lot more on. Perhaps that would work. I looked in my handbag – it wasn't there! All that I could find was that bottle with the fruitcake in it that I had made at the factory. I didn't care, I put it on. I used up half of the bottle. Then I went outside again.

As I was walking back to the table I almost ran into the waiter who had served us. He stopped and looked at me with a stupid look on his face. Then he remembered he had a job to do, walked on and knocked down a table with some cakes on it.

When I finally reached the table, Mr Amos was looking embarrassed, as if he didn't want to be seen with me. I could see he was trying to hide it but he couldn't. Suddenly a strange thing happened: he opened his mouth, as if he was going to speak, then stopped. He had smelled the perfume – the fruitcake special – that I was wearing, and the change that came over him was immediate. His look of embarrassment just disappeared. Instead, he looked like a dog who had just found a bone; his eyes shone and he smiled until I thought his face would break in two. He stood up.

'At last you're back – I missed you, Anna,' he said. 'I've been in a terrible dream and I've just woken up.'

'A dream, Mr Amos?' I asked. I didn't understand what he was talking about.

'Call me David, darling . . .' he said.

Darling? What did he mean? What was happening?

'Yes . . .' he continued. 'I dreamt that I was being awful to you, treating you as if you were just someone who worked for me. The truth is that you mean so much more than that to me . . .'

I wondered what he meant. Was he going to raise my pay?

He went on. 'You must realise that I'm crazy about you, darling.'

He was calling me *darling* again. He was being serious.

I have to say that at this point I was feeling very confused. Five minutes ago my boss didn't want to be seen with me. Now he was saying he was crazy about me! What could be making him behave like this? Then, all at once, I realised: it was the fruitcake special! *Intrigue* might smell great, but it didn't make a girl attractive to men. But my fruitcake perfume did.

'I feel my heart growing with love for you, Anna,' said Mr Amos. He was looking at my body through the black dress.

Just then a waitress came to the table. She told me that I had a telephone call and asked me to answer it in the lounge.

I wondered what it was about.

'Excuse me, David – I won't be long,' I said.

'A minute is a long time when you're gone, Anna,' he said. His words were like conversation from a bad movie. But I kept quiet about it – he was my boss, after all, even if he had gone crazy.

When I got to the lounge I took the phone. I noticed someone waving their arms at me from another phone across the large room. I could see it was that waiter again – there were bits of cake all over his trousers.

Now what could *he* want?

I soon found out.

'Miss . . .' his voice was excited at the other end of the line. '. . . I know I am only a poor waiter but love makes me brave . . .'

Why did everybody sound like bad movies tonight?

'When I saw you just now,' said the waiter, 'I couldn't stop myself from falling in love with you. You are so beautiful. Please tell me you will see me . . . I know I can offer you more than that rich fool you're sitting with. I may not have his money or his looks, but I love you far more than he ever could. Please be mine!'

'Wait a minute, Romeo,' I said. 'Why don't you just calm down and serve the lobster, like a good little waiter?'

It was the perfume, my fruitcake special again. The waiter had a good smell of it when he had passed by earlier and now he thought he was in love with me, the poor man. It wasn't his fault. I told him that if he loved me he would not talk loudly about it.

'Of course, my love. I will not embarrass you . . . darling!' the waiter said.

So far I'd had two men call me *darling* in one evening. Aunt Mimi would be pleased.

But if the perfume had worked in that way on the waiter, I had better take care not to pass by any other males too closely. I could end up with a group of men following me home, all saying they loved me. And wouldn't that be awful? Well, wouldn't it? Well, maybe not but it wouldn't be easy to explain to Momma. And I wouldn't even *mention* it to Aunt Mimi!

Thank goodness the place was quiet that night. I walked back to the table, trying my best to keep away from other men who were in the restaurant. I was lucky; it seemed that they would have to get close to the perfume to get the effects.

When I got back to the table I saw that David had been joined by Sabina, a beautiful young model who was his latest girlfriend – their pictures had been in all the papers recently.

'So, you're Anna. I haven't seen you before, Anna.' Sabina said my name as if it were a dirty word. 'Don't you work for David making perfume or something? Terribly exciting.'

She held out her hand to me as if I were expected to kiss it. I didn't.

'Sabina,' said David. 'Anna is the woman I love.'

I could hardly believe my ears. David Amos was telling me he loved me right under the nose of his beautiful girlfriend, Sabina. All because of my fruitcake. I had to say something. This was getting to be silly.

'David, I really think . . .' I began.

But at that moment our waiter made another

appearance. He was playing a guitar and singing 'O Sole Mio' to me at the top of his voice. Well, he did say he wouldn't *talk* loudly – I didn't say anything about *singing* loudly. I must remember next time.

As for Sabina, she didn't know whether to laugh or cry at the sight of two men both saying how much they loved me at the same time – and while *she* was there.

So she hit David in the face.

The waiter sang even louder than before. David hit him on the chin. As I moved away from the table, a fight developed between Sabina, David, the singing waiter and several more waiters who were trying to calm things down.

Soon the place was a loud, confused mess of cake, pieces of lobster, pools of wine and bits of broken guitar.

Time to go, I thought.

I ran downstairs and caught a taxi home. Thank goodness the taxi driver was a woman!

* * *

When I got home, Aunt Mimi had gone and Momma was asleep – she never could stay awake when she was excited. I had some quiet moments to think about what had happened. Why had my perfume had such an effect on men who would not normally take any notice of me? Nothing had been put in that was any different. Nothing, that is, except Aunt Mimi's fruitcake.

What a fruitcake!

Then I had a thought. What if I, as a chemist, could find out what it was in that fruitcake that caused men to go mad with love? People would pay a lot to know a thing like that. I could make a lot of money! There was no reason, come to think of it, why I should let Amos Cosmetics know about it. After all, it wasn't *their* fruitcake. But I couldn't do a thing unless I knew what was in the cake – and only Aunt Mimi knew that.

I decided to miss work the next day – I would say I had a cold or something. I also wanted to avoid David Amos who might still be affected by the fruitcake special, or the fight that had followed.

* * *

Aunt Mimi lived in a nice little apartment on the other side of town. I had gone out before Momma got up. I didn't want to be questioned about my 'new young man'. It took an hour to get there on the bus.

When at last I arrived Aunt Mimi gave me a warm welcome. Soon we were sitting in her kitchen, talking about this and that. We both knew what Aunt Mimi was going to ask me about in the end, so neither of us minded talking about other things first. Aunt Mimi was good company when she wasn't talking about husbands.

I mentioned the fruitcake.

'Anna,' said Aunt Mimi, 'I've known you since you were born and you've never baked a cake in your life. Now you want to know how to bake a fruitcake. What's going on?'

'Nothing, Aunt Mimi, I just thought the cake was delicious and wondered if I could bake one too. There's no harm in that, is there?' Of course, I was lying. We both knew it.

'So,' Aunt Mimi said. 'This new man of yours – he wants you to bake him a cake. Who does he think you are, his mother? Just what were you two doing last night, having a cookery class?'

'Oh, please, Aunt Mimi,' I begged. 'I really need to know. I promise that as soon as you tell me I'll tell you everything about last night.'

Aunt Mimi was interested. '*Everything*?'

'Everything,' I said. 'No secrets.'

Aunt Mimi smiled. 'Well, my dear, I hate to tell you this but I didn't make the cake. I bought it.'

'You bought it?' I said, unable to hide the surprise in my voice. '*Where* did you buy it?'

'From a little place in the market, the open-air one that takes place twice a week in the park. There's an old lady there who said she used to bake them for her husbands. She had *seven* of them, would you believe? And they all ate her fruitcakes.'

Somehow I wasn't surprised that she had had seven husbands. Not with those fruitcakes.

'Did she say what she put in them?' I asked, hopefully.

'Only that she put in a "special something" that she grew herself,' said Aunt Mimi. 'She wouldn't say what. She told me that she only baked that kind of cake a few times. As a matter of fact, she knew that I was thinking about finding a husband for you. I don't know how she knew but she did.

Anyway, this woman who made the cake told me to give it to you and your problems would be over. I didn't believe what she said, but I used to buy the fruitcakes because they were delicious.'

I noticed that Aunt Mimi was talking about this old lady

as if she wasn't around any more. I feared the worst. Was she dead?

'Can we see this old lady to ask her about it?' I asked.

Aunt Mimi looked at me sadly. 'I'm afraid she died last week – I went to her funeral. They say she was over a hundred years old. There were a lot of strangers there, not from around here, all speaking in some kind of strange way. They seemed to think she was important, though nobody ever took much notice of her around here.'

'Except you, Aunt Mimi,' I said.

Aunt Mimi smiled. 'Well, you know how I can't mind my own business.'

I knew.

'Speaking of which,' she said, moving closer to me, 'it's your turn.'

'My turn?' I asked.

'To tell me everything that happened last night,' she said.

And so I did. Everything, just as I had promised. I don't know whether Aunt Mimi believed me or not, but if she didn't she never let it show.

She's not a bad old lady, my Aunt Mimi. Not when you get to know her.

*   *   *

In the end I had two days off work. I said I'd been sick and in a way I was: I wouldn't feel well until I knew the truth about the fruitcake. I knew that there was little chance of discovering what actually went into it. I would have to work it out from the small amount I had left in the bottle. I had used up more than I thought the other night.

But I was not sure that I wanted to make my fortune

from the old woman's secret. Perhaps it was only right that the secret should lie buried with her.

Then again, perhaps not.

Momma seemed satisfied with my explanation that things had just not worked out between me and Mr Amos, although she thought it a wasted opportunity – she wanted me to have a rich husband. Still, happiness is what really counts, she said, with a note of sadness in her voice.

When I finally got back to the factory there was a message left on my desk – could I see Mr Amos as soon as I got in.

As I walked towards David Amos's office I felt like a schoolgirl who had to go to see the head teacher. I was sure that the fruitcake special would not still be working by now – after all, he had not seen me for a few days. I knocked on his door.

Mr Amos was sitting behind his big desk with a large black eye. Standing next to him, smiling and wearing dark glasses and a hat, was Sabina. She had her arm around his shoulders.

'I hope you are well now, Anna.' said Mr Amos.

'Yes, thank you, Mr Amos,' I said. (I thought calling him 'David' might not be the best thing to do at this point. I could see Sabina wasn't pleased to see me.) 'I hope you are well yourself,' I added quickly.

'My eye hurts a bit – your waiter could hit hard!' he said with a little smile.

So could Sabina, I thought, as I remembered how she had hit him. But I said nothing.

'Anyway,' Mr Amos said, 'I managed to calm them down so that there was no more trouble and the police were not called. Your waiter had been partly to blame, too, so they accepted my apologies – at a price, of course. At least the name of Amos Cosmetics didn't appear in the newspapers.

'And, as for that other matter of my strange behaviour towards you – I can't explain what affected me. I mean, a man like myself and a woman like . . . I mean . . .' he looked towards Sabina.

Sabina finished it off for him.

'He means that a rich and handsome man like him could not possibly fall in love with a nobody like you when he has a beautiful girl like me. Isn't that right, David?'

'You express it so well, darling,' he said.

Sabina continued: 'So David wants you to accept a bit of money to make up for any disappointments you may have had, then you can go back to making perfumes at the factory again. Right, David?'

'Absolutely, darling,' said Mr Amos before turning to me again. 'Well, Anna, I hope that has helped to . . . er . . . clear things up a little. I'm sorry there had to be this, er, confusion. I hope this has sorted things out between us.'

I stood watching Sabina smile as she put her fingers down his collar.

'Well, Mr David Amos,' I said, 'perhaps you can use your famous expert nose to sort this out, too!' I had reached into my handbag for something to throw when I saw Sabina laughing. I took the top off the first thing I found and threw everything that was in the bottle all over the front of Sabina's dress.

'Take that and him too, you horrible little woman!' I shouted.

When I looked at my hand it was holding the now empty bottle of fruitcake special. The room was already beginning to fill with its smell. I got out before Mr Amos lost control of himself again, out of the office and out of my career at Amos Cosmetics.

Sabina, of course, would now enjoy all the extra attention she would get from strange men, thanks to the fruitcake special. I'm not sure that Mr David Amos would enjoy the competition, though.

* * *

It happened sometime later, shortly after I had begun to work at the factory where they made *Intrigue*. I was trying to make a fruitcake (I mean you never know!) when Momma and I heard a knock at the door.

'Momma,' I said, 'if it's Aunt Mimi with news of another "perfect boy" for me, tell her I'm not interested.'

'It's not Aunt Mimi, dear,' said Momma.

'Who is it?' I asked.

'I think you'd better come see for yourself,' Momma said.

I went to the front door. It was Armstrong, the pizza delivery man. He was holding up a pizza box which had 'Armstrong's Peachy Pizzas' in big letters on the front.

Armstrong now owned the pizza company.

He explained that he'd fallen in love with me when he first delivered pizza to us, but he wanted to be a success before asking me out. He said I deserved no less. Then he gave me some flowers. I never really noticed before, but Armstrong is quite good looking: a bit short maybe, a little thin on top – but nobody's perfect.

'Momma, get the man a drink,' I said, enjoying his smile.

And the smell of fruitcake went past us and out the door.

The Real Aunt Molly

My Aunt Molly is the kindest, sweetest person on earth. She may not be the cleverest woman in the world, but I love her a lot. However, a strange thing happened to Aunt Molly and now we don't know what to do.

It all started when her husband, Uncle Dalton, died. Well, I called him Uncle Dalton but she always called him 'Dally'. He was my mother's only brother. Aunt Molly really loved him, we all knew that.

Life had been quite difficult for Aunt Molly when she was a child. She was poor and her parents had died early on. She was left to look after herself. She had never learned to read properly and left school at an early age. But she was always cheerful and honest and never complained about the hard work she did to earn her living. She worked as a cleaner wherever there was work to do. She liked cleaning because she didn't have to make any difficult decisions. Aunt Molly didn't like making decisions. Perhaps she wasn't used to it. I don't know. But everybody liked her and she was never out of work.

She met Uncle Dalton when she was working as a cleaner at the bus station. He was a bus driver and it was when he had just finished for the day that he first saw her cleaning the station office. He fell in love with her as soon as he saw her. It was the same for Aunt Molly. As soon as their eyes met it was love for both of them. He soon grew to love her gentleness and she loved his kind heart and willingness to make decisions.

They got married two weeks later.

A year after that she gave birth to twin boys. They were my cousins and their names were Winston and Clement. I was born in the same year two months later. I was called Rufus. I still am. Anyway, Uncle Dalton got a better job at the bus station soon afterwards, and they bought a house near us.

Aunt Molly and Uncle Dalton had a happy marriage. Uncle Dalton earned the money and Aunt Molly cooked, cleaned and made the house a wonderful home for her dear Dally and the boys.

It would not be quite right to say that Aunt Molly

actually *ran* the house. In fact, all the big decisions were left to Uncle Dalton. But she made sure that everything went smoothly. Everybody was happy. I was happy, too, because I liked to play with my cousins. I also looked forward to the delicious home-made biscuits Aunt Molly always gave me.

My cousins and I were five years old when Uncle Dalton was run over by a bus at the station. It was an accident. Uncle Dalton didn't know what hit him and he was killed immediately. Well, I suppose he guessed it was a bus, but I don't think he had much time to think it over, if you see what I mean. Anyway, he was dead.

In a way, once Uncle Dalton had died, I think a part of Aunt Molly died too. She was still a hard worker and remained a good mother to Winston and Clement. Indeed, the routine of running the house was something she no longer needed any help with. My parents and Uncle Dalton's parents – my grandparents – all helped Aunt Molly with the decision making. But the cheerfulness that we had come to expect from her had gone. It was as if all her cheerfulness had died with Uncle Dalton, her 'dear Dally'. She got some money from the bus company because Uncle Dalton had been killed at work. At least she didn't have to leave the twins in order to earn money.

Life continued.

The twins grew into fine boys. But by the time they were fourteen they wanted to see a bit more of the world outside their comfortable home. Both of them were bright and interested in the world outside. Especially Winston. They were beginning to get bored with life at home with all its safe routines.

That's where the trouble really began. Aunt Molly had not really changed since their father's death. She had not even learned to read properly. She never went out and had no outside interests. She spent what free time she had listening to the radio or watching the television, especially game shows.

The boys, though they loved their mother, wanted to decide more things for themselves. And like me, they wanted to go out more. Aunt Molly, however, just wanted to stay at home all the time. The boys never went out much with their mother – whenever they did go out, it was with me and my parents or with our grandparents. Aunt Molly always stayed at home.

It was Winston who thought of taking their mother to the theatre on her next birthday. She would be thirty-nine. The boys planned it all out carefully with the help of the rest of the family. We were all there, my parents and my grandparents.

'I don't think Mum would like to see a Shakespeare play or anything like that,' said Clement. 'But I'm sure that going to see *something* would do her good!'

'You're right,' said Gran. 'I think your mother should go to see something she would enjoy. It would make a nice change for her. Something like those shows she likes on the television.'

'Gran, you're brilliant!' said Winston. 'What about that show on the television with that hypnotist guy . . . the *Maxwell Marvel Show*? Mum loves that!'

'What's that all about?' asked Grandpa. 'I don't think I've seen it.'

'You must be the only person in the country who hasn't,'

said Clement. 'Maxwell Marvel is an expert hypnotist – he gives people suggestions and orders after he has made them go to sleep. When they wake up they do all kinds of funny things. Then, at an order from Maxwell Marvel, they go to sleep again. When they wake up again, they can't remember a thing about it.'

Grandpa laughed. 'I've had a few evenings like that myself.' Gran looked at him. 'Er . . . when I was much younger, of course,' he added quickly.

'Mum would really like to see that show – I just know it,' said Winston.

'Yes, but how do we get your Mum on a television show? Won't it be expensive? How will we get the money?' I asked.

'Relax,' said Winston. 'All we have to do is write to the television company and they'll send us the tickets free – that's where they get their live audiences from! All we have to do is make sure we let them know in time for the show.'

We all agreed that this was a great idea. So we did it. Aunt Molly, of course, was at first unwilling to go along with it. However, we had all made the decision for her and we wouldn't take no for an answer. In her heart, though, she did not really care what happened to her, not since her dear Dally had gone. But she went along to please her boys because she cared deeply for them, and did not want to disappoint them.

* * *

The television studio – the place where the show took place – was not at all what Aunt Molly imagined it would be like. She thought it would be like the inside of a theatre or a cinema. It wasn't. It was full of lighting and sound equipment. There were all kinds of people around whose job it was to make sure that everything worked properly. The audience itself was smaller than she expected. She could see the star of the show, Maxwell Marvel, nervously brushing his jacket in full view of the audience.

'Don't worry, Mum,' said Winston with confidence. 'It's always like this in a television studio. They're just getting ready for the show.'

Aunt Molly was sitting in the middle of the second row between the twins. I was there, too, along with Grandpa, who, from time to time, took little drinks from a small bottle of something he kept in his pocket. He was smiling.

Gran had stayed at home.

'Hey, the show's starting,' said Clement.

A man came out and told some jokes to make everybody feel more relaxed. He explained how the show was recorded for television and what was expected of the audience.

Then the lights went down and the opening music to the show started. Maxwell Marvel came into the centre of the studio, full of smiles. The audience clapped for a long time. Aunt Molly had seen this show many times on television, so she knew what to expect. Even so, we could tell that she was getting excited. We could see her smiling. It had been a long time since we had seen her smile like that. Then the show began.

Maxwell Marvel asked for some people from the audience to be hypnotised. Quite a few of the audience were willing but only about ten were chosen. They came on to the small stage and were immediately hypnotised by Maxwell.

They were told to do the strangest things – such as behaving like farm animals, or dancing at a disco, or acting like famous people. And they did everything they were told to do! Even the quiet looking ones were persuaded to do things that looked completely different from their usual behaviour.

Then, at a word or sign from Maxwell, they became themselves again and couldn't remember anything about what they had done. Some of them didn't even believe that they had been hypnotised at all and would only believe Maxwell after they were shown a video of what they had been doing.

Everybody loved it. Including Aunt Molly.

The final part of the show came when Maxwell asked for a last person to come forward.

'Here!' shouted Winston. He was pointing at his mother.

'Winston! What are you doing?' she said. 'I can't do that – I'd die of embarrassment!' Peinlichkeit

'Oh, go on, Mum. Do something different for once,' Clement whispered loudly. Grandpa and I were smiling. Aunt Molly smiled too.

She felt that she couldn't say no after all the trouble they had taken. What if she did look silly? That wouldn't matter. Nothing mattered now but her boys.

'All right – I'll do it!' she said.

Aunt Molly, for some reason, was an especially easy person to hypnotise. As she sat on a chair she 'went to sleep' to the sound of Maxwell's voice like a baby. We all wondered what hypnotic suggestions Maxwell would give her. Then Maxwell turned to Winston and said:

'What suggestions would you like to make, young man? I'll tell this lovely lady to do anything that won't get her into trouble with the police!'

The audience laughed.

The twins whispered to each other, then Winston spoke. 'Well . . . Mum's always needed a bit more confidence, so what could you do to make her more . . .'

'*Decisive*!' said Clement.

'That's it,' said Winston. 'More able to make decisions and be more confident – let her live life to the full!'

'Let's see what we can do,' said Maxwell. He first asked for her name and Grandpa told him. Then Maxwell turned to Aunt Molly who was still fast asleep. 'Now, Molly, you will answer only to my voice, do you understand?'

'I understand,' said Aunt Molly quietly, though she was still asleep.

'You will be a confident woman, full of strength. Whatever you want to do, you will succeed in doing. Nothing is too difficult for you. Is that clear to you, Molly?' said Maxwell.

Molly said that it was.

'When I tell you to open your eyes you will be that intelligent, confident woman; you will live life to the full. You will not remember that you have been hypnotised but you will be a new, confident woman who will live life to the full. You will continue until I – and only I – tell you to return to your normal life. Is that understood, Molly?' said Maxwell loudly and with quite a lot confidence of his own.

Molly said she understood.

'Now, Molly,' said Maxwell. 'Open your eyes . . .' But as

he said this he suddenly gave a loud cry and fell at Aunt Molly's feet while holding on to his tie. His face had turned grey. Maxwell Marvel had a heart attack just as Aunt Molly was opening her eyes.

The first thing she saw was Maxwell Marvel lying at her feet. She turned to the nearest person in the audience and said, 'Well, don't just sit there, man! This man has obviously had a heart attack – call for a doctor and an ambulance at once. He needs immediate attention.'

The man did as he was told while Aunt Molly undid Maxwell's tie and put him in a comfortable position. She acted as if she knew exactly what to do. Help soon arrived and the unconscious Maxwell was taken away in an ambulance.

A man from the television company spoke to the audience and explained that, because of Maxwell Marvel's sudden and unfortunate accident, the show was at an end. He said he was very sorry that things had been cut short in this way.

Somebody behind us called out that it had been the best part of the show.

Grandpa went up to the man who had spoken to us. He asked him what they could do to get Aunt Molly back to normal now that Maxwell Marvel wasn't here.

'You heard Maxwell,' the man told him. 'Only his voice can undo the orders. I'm sorry – you'll have to wait until Maxwell can speak to her himself.'

'But what if . . .' asked Grandpa, '. . . what if he doesn't get better?'

'Let's all hope that he does,' the man said. 'It's a popular show. Anyway, the order he gave her wasn't so bad was it?

It's not as if he told her to start acting like a monkey or something! Don't worry – we'll get in touch.'

* * *

In the car on the way back home we talked about what had happened that evening. We had all been surprised, to say the least, at the way Aunt Molly had behaved when Maxwell Marvel had had his heart attack; she had been more in control than anybody. It was as if she had known exactly what to do.

'Nonsense,' said Aunt Molly when we put this to her. 'just a little common sense. Besides, everything about his condition showed that his attack was not a serious one. He should get better soon if he rests for a while and looks after himself.'

Was this Aunt Molly talking? We could hardly believe what we were hearing. She sounded like a doctor.

'How do you know that, Mum?' asked Winston.

'I heard a radio programme all about looking after your heart – it described everything about heart conditions very clearly,' she answered.

'And when, exactly, did you hear this?' asked Grandpa.

'Oh, ten years ago while I was cleaning the carpet. When Dally was alive. Bless him,' said Molly with a smile.

* * *

The week that followed Aunt Molly's return home was full of surprises for all of us. She was not the Molly we all knew. For a start, she soon discovered that she could read, after all. After years of hardly looking at even a newspaper, she began to read anything she could get her hands on. At first it was cheap magazines and love stories. Then she started on serious newspapers and Russian novels.

During the following weeks she took up painting and found that she was able to paint beautiful pictures. Soon she could paint as well as a professional. Then her beloved cooking changed. No longer did she cook simple but delicious meals. Now she tried Indian, Chinese and Italian meals which were also, it must be said, delicious.

She started to go out to all kinds of places – museums, art shows, scientific talks given by experts, political meetings – and she took the twins, too!

'You were complaining that we never went out – we're going out!' she said to them.

Nobody dared to advise her any more.

'I'm a grown woman – I can do things for myself, thank you very much!' she would tell us.

Then she came home with Horace, the Professor of Classics at the university. He was an expert on ancient Greek and Roman history.

'Horace has asked me to spend a week in Greece with him. We're going to explore the ancient buildings,' she said.

'But Mum . . .' began the twins.

'No buts . . .' Molly said. 'I'd rather explore an ancient building than look like one. Besides, Horace is a good-looking man – with brains, too. He likes me. And I'm still an attractive woman; I could marry again. It's about time I started to live life to the full. I've stayed at home for too long.'

We were all amazed by this new Aunt Molly. She could,

it seemed, do anything she put her mind to. And although we loved the old Aunt Molly, we soon liked this new person who had come into our lives.

In fact, she was now a lively, funny and thoughtful woman. She scared us a little, too, with her burning wish for improvement.

But we all found her very, very easy to like.

* * *

It was twelve weeks after Maxwell Marvel had had his heart attack. We had heard nothing from him but we saw on the television that he had been let out of hospital.

Two days after he left hospital he was found dead in the bed of his latest twenty-year-old girlfriend. He had died of another heart attack. He was forty-nine.

A week after Maxwell Marvel's death, Grandpa received a letter from the man he had spoken to at the television studio. There was a taped message with the letter. On the tape was a recording of Maxwell giving the order for Aunt Molly to return to what she had been before. He had recorded the message just before he left hospital, just before he hurried off to meet his new lover.

* * *

It has now been a week since Grandpa got the letter.

We still haven't played the tape to Aunt Molly. We can't decide what we should do.

We have discovered another person in Aunt Molly and we love her, too. She's a new Aunt Molly who has rediscovered life. Yet we also love and miss the sweet, kind lady who raised the twins. The old Aunt Molly.

The truth is, we don't know which Aunt Molly is now the real one. What would happen if we played her the tape? Would a part of her die once again, as it had seemed to do when Uncle Dalton died? Would it be right for us to take this new life away from her? Then, again, perhaps nothing would happen and she would remain as she is – full of the love of life.

And which Aunt Molly has the most right to be here – the old or the new?

Who is the real Aunt Molly?

She and Horace are going off to Greece next week. That will give us all time to think things over. Then we will decide.

The old or the new?

Well, what would *you* do?

Brains

The small monkey carefully completed the last piece of the one-hundred-piece puzzle. When all the pieces of the puzzle were put together, they made a copy of *Sunflowers*, a picture by the famous painter, Van Gogh.

'Well done, Max!' said a young woman in a white coat. 'It only took you twenty minutes this time – that's much better than the last time you tried it. Have a bite of lovely banana.'

The woman reached for the fruit from a bowl close by and gave it to the monkey. Max ate it happily. The woman's name was Gina Capaldi and she was twenty-six years old. She was studying for a Ph.D. at a university in Rome. She was hoping to become a Doctor of Science. Her ideas had already caused much excitement. Now her work was almost finished. Great things were expected of her.

As Gina prepared the monkey's next drug, Max played with his Rubik cube. The Rubik cube was one of Max's favourite puzzles. He enjoyed turning around the sides of the cube in his hands so that each of the six sides was a different colour. Gina looked over at him and was pleased. He was getting better every day.

Max completed the Rubik cube in five minutes.

* * *

Mr Dimitri sat behind a big desk in a large office in a huge building in New York. On the front of his desk was a sign in gold letters which read: *Mr Theodore Dimitri.* On his door there was a much bigger sign which read: *President of the Centre for Science and Business Development* (CSBD).

Mr Dimitri was middle-aged and wore a large dark-grey suit. He smoked a thick expensive cigar. The smoke from his cigar filled the room.

Today he was going to see his most promising new scientists. They were all studying for Ph.D.s so that they could become Doctors of Science. They had to give him their new ideas if they wanted money from the CSBD. Mr Dimitri did this every year. If he liked their work, CSBD would give them lots of money to develop it. That was the way to make money in the future.

And Mr Dimitri was good at making money.

But if he didn't like the work of these scientists, or if he didn't like them, he didn't have to give them a cent. 'After all,' Mr Dimitri thought, 'Business is business.'

Miss Epstein, his secretary, came into his office.

'Miss Capaldi to see you, Mr Dimitri, sir,' she said.

'Send her in, Miss Epstein,' said Mr Dimitri in a voice which was cold and business-like.

Gina Capaldi stood in her best suit and shoes in front of the big desk. She wanted to look her best before Mr Dimitri. In her bag was all the information needed about her work. She felt ready.

'Do sit down, Miss Capaldi. I've heard so many good things about you,' said Mr Dimitri in a voice that now sounded friendly and welcoming.

'Thank you, Mr Dimitri,' said Gina. She sat down in front of the big desk. Then Miss Epstein seemed to appear out of nowhere with coffee and biscuits. She put them on the desk and was gone again.

'Allow me,' said Mr Dimitri, as he put his cigar down for a moment and poured the coffee.

Gina took her coffee and left the biscuits. She didn't feel like eating. She was nervous. Mr Dimitri smiled at her with teeth that were large and white. Perfect teeth. His cigar found its way back to his mouth. The smoke rose up.

'Tell me, Gina . . . may I call you Gina?' he asked.

'Of course, Mr Dimitri,' she answered.

Mr Dimitri continued. 'Tell me about your latest work; I've heard very interesting things about it, but I would like you to explain it clearly to a simple man such as myself.'

Gina knew that Theodore Dimitri was far from being

simple. You don't get to be the head of CSBD, the biggest organisation of its kind, if you aren't very clever. She knew his decision could change her life.

Gina began: 'I've discovered a drug which raises intelligence.'

'Hold on, Gina!' said Mr Dimitri. 'You mean to say you've found a way of making people smarter?'

'Yes,' Gina answered. 'And without any harmful side effects as far as I can tell . . .'

'As far as you can tell?' Mr Dimitri said, his eyebrows raised.

'I mean,' said Gina, 'the work has not been used on people – I've only worked on animals. Especially Max.'

'Max?' asked Mr Dimitri.

'Sorry – Max is a monkey,' Gina explained.

'A monkey . . .' said Mr Dimitri but his voice sounded less friendly than it had before.

Gina knew she had to persuade him somehow. 'Max has done really well – it's quite amazing. He now has the intelligence of an eight-year-old human child. He can do many things . . .'

'You want money for a performing monkey?' said Mr Dimitri. He sounded a little annoyed. 'I can go to any cheap show to see smart monkeys doing tricks. And I don't have to pay a lot of money for it, either.'

'Mr Dimitri,' Gina said as she reached for her bag, 'I have a video of Max. I think you should see it before you make any decisions.'

'Oh, you do?' His voice was lower – not a good sign.

'Yes,' said Gina. 'If you would allow me. I'm sure you'll be as excited as I am once you've seen it.' Gina did not want to give up without a fight. Her future depended on Mr Dimitri's decision.

'Let's see what you've got,' he said in his low voice.

The video showed Max three years earlier, before Gina had begun to work on him when he was still a normal monkey. Then, three months after her work had begun, Max was seen drawing simple pictures with a pencil. After a year he was spelling out simple words. After two years he could add and take away simple numbers. After three years he could read, write and do basic mathematics. He also understood everything Gina said to him. Max had come to see Gina as his mother and he loved her. The video finished with Max putting his arms around Gina while Gina laughed.

'That's one smart monkey. Can you make him any smarter?' Mr Dimitri asked.

Gina knew he was interested. She was pleased.

'Max can be as intelligent as we want to make him, Mr Dimitri,' she said, trying not to show her pleasure in what she had achieved.

'Yes,' he said. 'But could that monkey be made to be as smart as a man?'(Or a woman, thought Gina)

'As I said, Mr Dimitri,' said Gina, 'we can make him as intelligent as we want to.'

'You mean,' asked Mr Dimitri, 'that that monkey could get to be smarter than I am?'

'I suppose it is possible – there's no reason why not, as far as I can tell. Although, of course, Max is a long way from that just now,' Gina said.

'But you're working on it, right?' Mr Dimitri asked.

'Well, er . . . yes.' Gina was less confident now.

'And what if you worked on a human being – could you make them smarter?' he asked.

Gina answered: 'I think so, Mr Dimitri.'

Mr Dimitri narrowed his eyes. 'You only think so?'

'Well,' said Gina, 'the brains of a monkey and a man are built in much the same way, so I'm almost certain.'

'*Almost* certain. Hmm . . .' Mr Dimitri looked out of the window, down at the streets of the busy city far below them. His cigar smoke rose lazily to the ceiling.

Gina's hopes of money and success – and her Ph.D. – depended largely on the decision Mr Dimitri would make.

'Tell me, Miss Capaldi . . .' said Mr Dimitri.

Gina noticed he had stopped using her first name. This looked bad.

'. . . have you ever taken this stuff yourself to increase your own intelligence?' With that, he turned to look out of the window again.

'Of course not, Mr Dimitri,' Gina said to the back of his head. 'But if you think I should . . .'

'NO!'

Mr Dimitri had turned suddenly from the window as he said this. The speed of his action surprised her because he was such a large man. His eyes were wide and looked angry. Gina was scared.

'Miss Capaldi,' Mr Dimitri said, lowering his voice, 'your work has been very good. In fact, it has been excellent and you have my congratulations. Unfortunately, I must ask you to stop what you are doing. At once.'

Gina's mouth suddenly felt very dry and she felt the hairs on her head rise up.

'But Mr Dimitri,' she said, 'I've done so much . . . all my work, my Ph.D!'

'Who is going to believe you if they wonder for one moment if you took some of this stuff yourself?' Mr Dimitri's voice softened. 'They would say that anybody could get a Ph.D. with your wonder drug to help them. And they'd be right.'

'But I never . . . I mean . . . I wouldn't dream of doing such a thing!' said Gina. She tried not to show the disappointment she felt.

'Wouldn't you?' said Mr Dimitri. 'There are many people that would take this stuff. And many that would think that *you* had, too.'

Gina looked alarmed, but said nothing.

'Yes,' he continued, 'it's a sad fact but a true one. Many people would think that you had taken your own drug to make yourself smarter. They would see you as being no different to those athletes who take stuff they're not supposed to take. It might make them do better but it's not honest, is it, Miss Capaldi? And it's no different for CSBD – we do not want people to think that we are anything other than a completely honest organisation. If they ever thought we had anything to do with such behaviour they would never trust us again!'

'But I promise you . . . my work has all been done honestly,' said Gina. 'I never took anything!'

'But,' said Mr Dimitri as he looked straight at Gina's eyes, 'you would if I asked you to, wouldn't you?'

Gina knew it was true, so she said nothing and looked at the floor.

Mr Dimitri turned his great weight towards her and put his hand on her shoulder.

'I understand how much you want to succeed, Miss Capaldi. Don't worry . . . I'm going to talk to the people at your university – I think you should have a Ph.D. for the work you've done so far . . .'

Gina raised her eyes.

'Yes, Miss Capaldi, I believe in your honesty and believe you are a brilliant young scientist. I would very much like you to continue to work for us . . .'

Gina shut her eyes. She was too happy to speak.

'. . . but in a different area,' Mr Dimitri added.

Gina opened her eyes. She could hardly believe what she had heard.

'But what about my work?' she asked.

'You may carry on if you wish,' said Mr Dimitri, 'but you will have no money from us if you do. And I think I can say that nobody else will help you if I have anything to say about it – and I will.'

Gina felt bad about losing her work. But she had been offered a job – and her Ph.D.

'If you leave all your work with us, Miss Capaldi, we'll make sure that it is properly taken care of. After all, you have made a discovery which could change the world someday. And you can be sure that we will recognise you as the person behind it all when the time comes. But it could take a long time.

'But right now we would like to use your clever brain to the full in doing important work for us. And, of course, you will be safe in the knowledge that you have the CSBD behind you. You will never be short of money again. So why not join us, Gina? What do you say?'

Gina felt surprisingly good about the offer.

'And I'll get recognition for my work?' Gina asked.

'Definitely,' said Mr Dimitri.

'Mr Dimitri, I accept!'

There were smiles and goodbyes and, soon after, a happy Gina Capaldi left the room.

Mr Dimitri sat down, lit another cigar and watched the smoke rise up to the ceiling before it finally disappeared. He knew that business was not good when people asked too many questions. If people were made to be too smart they would do just that. And once they didn't get the answers they wanted, they might not buy things. And if they didn't buy things there would be no money to be made.

No-one would like that. No-one at all.

Miss Capaldi's work would be put away somewhere nice and safe. Somewhere secret. Along with all the other dangerous ideas. Like the car that ran on water, or the shoes that never wore out, or the battery that never stopped.

But he was glad to have Miss Capaldi. She was bright. He ought to give her something to do. Something that would make a lot of money. He picked up his telephone.

'Miss Epstein . . . See that Miss Capaldi is sent to the biological science centre. I want her to be a part of that three-legged chicken plan. She can do it, if anybody can. She's one smart lady. Oh, and Miss Epstein . . .'

'Yes, Mr Dimitri?' said Miss Epstein.

'I want you to see that a dangerous animal from one of our centres is killed. It's a monkey. His name is Max.'

The Book of Thoughts

Chester was feeling more tired than usual after a hard day at the office. He had joined the company only two years before. He had come straight from university then, but now he was a junior manager in one of the biggest companies in Singapore. It was an important position to have and meant lots of extra work.

He could understand the jealousy that some of the other workers might feel against the 'new boy', as they still called him. He had risen quickly in the company. Many of them, however, had been there for years doing the same jobs. He could understand how bad feeling towards him might lie hidden behind their smiles.

But it didn't make life any easier.

He needed people whose advice he could trust when he had to make difficult decisions. He had to be sure that the bad feelings of the other workers didn't get in the way of the important business decisions he had to make. He knew he would never become a manager unless he could be sure of people.

Then there was Dorothy.

Chester was fairly sure of his own good looks. He was dark and slim and dressed smartly, but with an eye to fashion. He was a confident speaker and believed himself to be a sociable and effective junior manager.

But when it came to Dorothy his judgement disappeared. Dorothy was a bright girl who had just joined the company, straight from university. He was attracted at once by her intelligent eyes, her shy, pretty face and her soft, round figure.

Ah, Dorothy!

Take today, for example. He had been given some new figures to check and he had asked Dorothy to read some of the details to him while he took notes. It was not until she had left that he realised that he had not written notes at all. Instead he had written Dorothy's name several times. He was too embarrassed to ask Dorothy for the details again, so he had to look them up in the office of old Mr Shaw.

Mr Shaw was known for always being in a bad mood and he was no different this time. He didn't like having to stay late to check figures for some junior manager. He didn't like it at all.

Chester hated it when he made mistakes. It didn't look good. But it didn't happen often.

He decided he would walk home instead of taking the train. It was late in the evening but he felt he needed the walk to clear his thoughts after a busy day. Anyway, it would be a little punishment for being so stupid earlier on. He decided that he would eat at the shopping centre near his home. He liked the Chinese food there.

As he walked towards his favourite Chinese restaurant, he saw that the lights were still on in an old antique shop. He had often thought of looking into this shop because he liked shops that sold old things. He stopped and looked. There were boxes full of old books piled outside the shop. On the shop window was a notice. It read: *Sorry, shop closed today. Open again tomorrow.*

He bent down to look at the books. He saw all the usual old books: school books, cookery books and other books with dirty, yellowing pages that were of no value to him. There was one small, old book, however, that he noticed at once. It looked much older than the rest of the books. He picked it up.

'Take it!' said a voice behind him. Chester turned to see a man of about eighty years old. The man had opened the shop door and was carrying another box full of old books. 'These have all been around for years. My nephew is taking over the business and I don't want to leave him with all this rubbish. Nobody wants to buy any of it, so take what you want – go on, help yourself!'

'Thanks,' said Chester as he put the old book into his jacket pocket and went on to the Chinese restaurant.

* * *

Chester sat at his table drinking a beer. He had been looking forward to his chicken and rice. When it arrived, he found that the chicken had not been cooked properly. It was pink inside. He decided to complain and called the waiter.

'Sir?' asked the waiter.

Chester noticed that the waiter was new to the place.

'I'm not eating this,' Chester told him. 'The chicken is pink inside – it hasn't been cooked properly.'

'It's rare chicken, sir,' the waiter said. 'Many of our customers prefer its finer taste.'

Chester looked straight at the waiter. He thought the waiter was not showing him enough respect.

'Really?' answered Chester.

'It's very popular, sir,' said the waiter.

'And I suppose the illness they caught from eating undercooked chicken was popular with them too, eh?' said Chester. Other people in the restaurant could hear. He was annoyed.

The waiter said nothing but his face turned red.

'Please take this chicken back,' Chester told the waiter, 'and give me a piece that has been cooked all the way through.'

'Certainly, sir,' said the waiter as he took the food and went back to the kitchen.

While Chester was waiting for his meal to return he remembered the little book in his pocket. He thought he would have a look at it while he was waiting. He took it out of his pocket and examined it.

It was small enough to fit easily into his pocket and was covered with old, fine leather. He had to clean off some of the dirt in order to read the title on the cover. At first the title seemed to be in another language with strange letters and shapes, but as he looked they seemed to change into English. He closed his eyes tightly and opened them again. He was mistaken, of course. He must have been. When he looked again the title of the book was there. It was still dirty but it was clearly written in English. It read: *The Book of Thoughts.*

It didn't say who wrote the book.

Chester thought it must be one of those old books which offered advice about life. He felt disappointed.

He tried to open the book but it had an old metal lock which stopped him. Then suddenly the book seemed to open quite naturally at the middle pages. It was almost as if it wanted him to read it.

What he saw when he looked surprised him. The pages had nothing written on them and they were clean and white, not at all like the yellowed pages one would expect to find in a book this old. Did all the pages have no writing on them?

Just then the waiter returned with Chester's chicken and rice and placed it before him.

'Thank you,' said Chester.

'My pleasure, sir,' answered the waiter with a smile.

Chester happened to look at the opened book. It now had writing on the pages which only a moment before had been clean and white. The writing said:

He wouldn't look so pleased with himself if he knew what I had put on to his chicken while I was in the kitchen. That will teach him to make me look silly.

Chester couldn't believe what he saw. Was this what the waiter was thinking?

'Anything else, sir?' asked the waiter politely.

'Er . . . no, thank you,' said Chester.

As the waiter walked off the writing disappeared. Chester looked at his meal. He didn't feel hungry any more. And he could hardly complain to the manager about the waiter. Not without telling them about the book. Who would believe him?

Chester left the chicken and rice alone, paid his bill and went. He did not leave the waiter a tip.

* * *

When Chester got home he felt exhausted. He took out the book and looked inside it once more. The pages were now all white and clear again. Perhaps it had all been a result of his tiredness. He had been thinking too much about work – and about Dorothy. That must be it. There was no other possible explanation: he was simply too tired to think straight.

He went to bed and slept almost at once.

* * *

The train was less crowded than usual the following morning. He was lucky enough to find a seat for his short journey. He liked to watch people as they all sat or stood with faces that gave no sign of what they were thinking. Everybody avoided looking at another person in the eye – that might cause trouble.

Chester relaxed in his seat. He had decided that the experience of the night before was best forgotten. Who ever heard of a book that read thoughts? The whole idea was crazy!

Then he remembered that he still had the book in his

pocket. He ought to throw it away in the next rubbish bin. Yes, that's what he would do. Get rid of the stupid thing.

He noticed that the woman who sat opposite was an attractive, smartly dressed middle-aged lady. Her eyes looked down and her face showed nothing of her thoughts. Chester wondered what she was thinking.

Should he look at the book?

Perhaps just a little look would be fun. Where was the harm in it?

He reached for the book in his pocket. He took it out.

'Go on,' he said to himself, 'you might as well try out the book. Just for a laugh. Do it!'

He opened the book and almost at once words in clear black letters appeared on the white pages. The words read:

I've given the best years of my life to him. Bank managers have married their secretaries before now. He must decide today – leave that awful wife and marry me or I'll shoot him and myself dead.

Chester saw that the woman's soft handbag had something in it that looked hard. Could it be a gun? He quickly shut the book and looked away.

Next he saw a tough-looking man wearing a T-shirt, showing his powerful arms. What was *he* thinking?

Chester opened the book. It read:

I like chicken better than pork. Fried chicken is the best. Followed by chocolate ice cream – my favourite. Mum's a great cook – I love you, Mum.

Chester couldn't help smiling at the man. The man saw him and gave him a dangerous look. Just then the train reached Chester's station.

Time to get off the train.

He closed the book and put it back into his pocket. As he walked the short distance to his office his mind turned from the book to Dorothy. He had been thinking of asking her out to dinner.

'I'll do it today,' he thought. 'But what if she hasn't thought about me in that way? Maybe she isn't as attracted to me as I am to her?'

For a moment his heart felt heavy.

'Hey, come on, Chester – she's not blind. She's sure to be interested – after all, you're a good-looking guy and you are a junior manager.'

* * *

Chester walked into his office. His secretary was already busy typing.

'Any messages, Miss Han?' he asked her.

'Yes, sir,' said Miss Han, 'from the Manager. He says he can't go to the meeting today about the Eastern business. He wants you to take over right away.'

Yes!

This was the kind of opportunity he'd been waiting for. He would show them all just how good he was. This was an important piece of business. If he could make sure that everything went well he would get noticed. He would be an obvious choice for the next manager's job. If he became a manager he would be the youngest manager in the business!

And Dorothy would like that, wouldn't she? What woman wouldn't?

He thought of her soft figure in his arms. Her voice was whispering his name softly, *Oh, Chester . . . Chester . . .*

Ah, Dorothy!

'No problem,' he told Miss Han. 'Tell the others I'll be there to prepare for the meeting in half an hour.'

* * *

When he met the others Chester was confident and did his job well. He made sure that everybody knew what to do. The meeting that afternoon was sure to be a success. If, of course, the figures he had were all correct.

Just then he noticed a little smile on the face of Mr Shaw.

'What's the old man got to smile about?' thought Chester. 'He never smiles – why is he smiling now?'

Then he remembered his little book.

He took it out of his pocket and hid it behind some papers. He pretended to be looking at his notes and thought of Mr Shaw. The words appeared immediately:

I'll teach that young fool a lesson. I've got some figures he doesn't know about hidden in my office. I've been working on this longer than he has. When he can't come up with the right figures he'll look stupid. Then I'll produce them and save the day. He'll look like a boy trying to do a man's job. He needs to learn some respect for experienced professionals like me.

Chester felt a cold sweat on the back of his neck.

'So the old man really does dislike me, after all!'

Chester wondered what all the others thought about him but had no time to consult his book.

'Thanks everybody – see you all this afternoon,' Chester told them all. 'Enjoy your lunch.'

* * *

While Mr Shaw was eating his sandwiches in the park, as he always did, Chester spent his lunch hour looking for the missing figures in Mr Shaw's office. Shaw was old-fashioned and preferred to use paper rather than recording things on a computer. It was a simple matter to copy the figures then leave Shaw's copies where he had found them – in a box in a cupboard. Chester felt almost disappointed. This was too easy!

Chester had missed his lunch but it had been worth it. His little book was turning out to be most useful.

*   *   *

The meeting that afternoon was a great success. He had all the figures he needed. The Eastern company people were happy and the papers were signed. Chester's future looked good. And as for Shaw . . . well, Chester could tell from his red face that he was angry because his little plan had gone wrong.

Chester made himself a promise: he would make sure that Shaw's future would *not* be good. Not if he could help it.

Chester did not like to lose.

After the meeting there would be just enough time to call in on Dorothy. Perhaps she would like to congratulate him over a drink.

When he got to her desk he found that she was away on a training course. She would be back the next day.

Just my bad luck, thought Chester.

Ah, well; for the time being he could find somebody else to share this happy time with. But how and who with?

Squash! It was his favourite game. Why not arrange a

game with Kim, his younger brother? Kim was a salesman. He had not gone to college but he had, like Chester, moved to the city. Chester always beat Kim at squash. He liked playing with Kim. He would telephone him as soon as he got home and see if a game could be arranged for that very night.

* * *

'Yeah . . . mmm . . . I see.'

Chester was in his apartment speaking on his mobile telephone. As he spoke he held the telephone more tightly than usual. He was listening to Kim. Kim was telling him that he had already promised to take his girlfriend to the cinema. As he spoke, Chester tried out the book to see if it would work over the telephone.

It did. It read:

I hate it when Chester and I play squash – he always wants to beat me. But he's always wanted to be a winner, at home, at school – it never stops, even when he has a career of his own. He never thinks of me, but then he never was much of a brother. He can do without his game this time. I'm staying home to watch television.

'OK, Kim,' said Chester. 'Enjoy the film. Yes . . . goodbye.'

Chester had never realised that his brother felt like that towards him. It came as a shock.

He spent the evening watching television and drinking wine with a takeaway meal.

At least, he thought, he would see Dorothy tomorrow.

* * *

The next morning Chester was sitting on his train to work. He was wondering whether he should look at *The Book of Thoughts* again when he noticed a photograph of the attractive middle-aged woman he had seen the day before. It appeared on the front page of a newspaper held open by the person sitting opposite him. Her picture was next to that of an older man. The headline read: TWO DIE IN LOVERS' SHOOTING.

He didn't have to read any more. It was obvious that the book had correctly read the woman's mind the day before and that she had carried out her plan. But it was too late to do anything now.

Anyway, it was none of his business.

Chester didn't feel like looking at the book for the rest of the journey. However, he did start to think more about the book. Why, he wondered, had he not told anyone else about it?

The truth was that he could hardly believe in it himself. If he started telling others about an amazing book that could read thoughts they would think he was crazy. And what harm might it do to his career? In any case, he did not know whether it would work for other people. Perhaps the book only worked for him.

'Best leave the book alone for now,' thought Chester. 'Yes, that would be best.'

But the book still sat in his pocket as he walked off the train.

* * *

The first part of the morning was brilliant. The Manager was very happy indeed with the way Chester had arranged the meeting with the Eastern company. It had been a great success. He received congratulations from all the people at the office. Many fine words were said to him about his bright future. Chester felt very pleased with himself.

Then he thought of his book.

What were they all *really* thinking about him? He wanted to know who he could trust and who he couldn't. He couldn't trust Shaw, he knew that. But, surely, there were not many like him. 'After all,' thought Chester, 'I am young, good-looking, cheerful, successful – and I'm one of the rising stars of the company. I must be one of the most popular guys here!'

But he wasn't.

In fact, the book told him so every time he looked at it. At first he thought it was only the older people who were jealous of his success. But it was the young ones, too. All of them. They thought he was clever but believed himself better than they were: good-looking but without any feelings. Some even thought he might be dishonest.

They hated him.

Chester had a lonely lunch at a café near the park. As he sat at his table, drinking strong coffee, he took out the book and looked at its cover. He read it: *The Book of Thoughts*.

He opened it. There was nothing there. Not a word. He wondered why it didn't show his own thoughts. Maybe it was because he already knew them. Maybe.

But what if he asked it to show him his deepest thoughts, the ones he didn't realise he was thinking? Would it do that? Should he ask it?

The idea frightened him. If thoughts were hidden,

perhaps there was a good reason for it. Yet he still wanted to look. It was almost too much for him.

'I won't do it!' he told himself. 'The last time I looked in the book it told me things I wish I hadn't found out. No, I won't do it! . . . Not yet.'

The café was becoming crowded so Chester walked back to the office.

Back to Dorothy.

She would be back from her training course by now. He would see her and ask her to dinner. He was certain that she would not be like the other people in the office.

His darling Dorothy.

* * *

When Chester got back to the office he saw Dorothy. She was talking to old Shaw. But Dorothy was nice to everybody. She was that kind of person. He called her over and she smiled to him. Even Shaw smiled.

Chester took her to a quieter part of the office and asked. Dorothy said yes, she would love to go to dinner with him. Her intelligent eyes were shining in her lovely face. Chester watched as her soft, round figure walked back to her desk.

Dorothy, at least, liked him. He could be sure of her.

Darling Dorothy!

But he would have just one quick look in the book to make sure.

He reached into his pocket. The book was not there. He felt alarmed. He quickly went back to his office. He searched all his pockets and his briefcase, even his desk drawers, though he knew he hadn't put the book in any of them. It was no use. *The Book of Thoughts* was gone.

Chester remembered the crowds as he left the café. Had somebody taken the book out of his pocket? Things don't just disappear by themselves.

Do they?

All kinds of thoughts crowded through his mind. But the least expected and perhaps the most welcome thought was the feeling that a heavy weight had been taken away from him. He went back to try and see Dorothy again. She was talking to old Shaw – again. She saw Chester and waved to him.

At least, he thought, he still had Dorothy.

He had his career and he had Dorothy. None of the other people mattered. He could trust Dorothy. Of course he could. He was almost sure of it . . .

Finders Keepers

Harry Chen looked like a middle-aged teacher. He always wore a tie and an old cotton jacket, even in the hot sun. His hair was going thin and he did not stand up straight. He was fifty years old and for the past twenty years had been a lecturer in archaeology at a university in Singapore.

He was also a thief.

His great love in life had always been archaeology. He loved to see things that had been hidden from human sight for hundreds, even thousands, of years. He loved the feeling of excitement he got when he held a piece of history in his hands. But his special love was pottery, the older the better.

Sometimes the university sent him to places where old pottery had been discovered. It was his job to sort out these things. The university would then put the things that were interesting in a museum where they could be shown to the public. But Harry Chen had his own private museum that nobody else knew about. He hated the idea of not keeping some of the old and, sometimes, beautiful things he found. And, if those beautiful things were only small things that nobody but he had seen, who would ever know if they were gone? So he kept them.

He had quite a collection of stolen things now, all carefully hidden in his home. They were mostly small, broken things that were not of much value. Even so, he did have some pots, rings and other favourite things that were extraordinary and lovely to see. He loved them so much he would sometimes, during the warm evenings, lay them all out on the floor to look at. He would examine each piece with love and care. Only he, he was sure, could understand their true value.

He lived alone in an old house which looked over the Singapore River. It was close to the antique shops which sold the old things he loved. He would often look in the shop windows at the beautiful things he could not afford to buy. Not on his salary. It made him angry to think that such things would end up in the home of some fat tourist who could not possibly see their true value as he could.

It wasn't fair.

* * *

Harry was looking forward to today. A very large old grave had been discovered while some forest land was being cleared. The university had been given the job of examining the grave and the things inside it. The grave was inside a big stone room which seemed to have been built for it.

'It's all a bit of a mystery so far, Harry,' said Professor Teo, Harry's head of department. 'The grave seems to be older than anything we'd expect to find on the island. It's definitely Chinese but I can't imagine whose grave it is.'

Harry was extremely interested. Perhaps there would be something for him to add to his collection.

'What would you like me to look at, Professor Teo?' asked Harry.

'Well, Harry,' answered the Professor, 'there's a few old bits – pots, vases and such like – which were found close to the body. They seem to be important but we aren't sure why yet. Perhaps you could see what you can find out.'

'No problem, Professor,' said Harry. 'I'll look into it.'

Soon the old pots were in Harry's room at the university and he was left alone to examine them. He loved this part of his work best of all.

He could see almost immediately that the pots were ancient. After carefully cleaning them he could see that most of them had contained perfumes and other valuable materials which were suitable for the grave of an important person. All of these things had long since lost their smell. Everything about them was dry, old and dead: there was nothing that made any of the pots different from hundreds of pots he had seen before. Harry was disappointed. There was nothing worth taking. Nothing.

He decided to clear up.

As Harry turned, he did something he had never done before – he knocked over one of the pots and broke it. He was annoyed with himself for being so careless and bent down to pick up the pieces.

The pot had been very plain and tightly shut up. All of the other pots had open tops. But not this one. Now that it was broken he could see that there had been something inside. It was a small, thin pipe about the length of his little finger. It was made of clay – the same stuff as the pots. He picked it up. It looked like a musical instrument, some kind of whistle for a child to blow into, perhaps? It might have some interest.

Harry decided the whistle would be worth taking home to look at. He put it into the pocket of his cotton jacket.

He told his professor about the broken pot but not about his whistle. He already thought about it as being *his* whistle.

'That's too bad,' said Professor Teo, 'but I don't suppose it was of much importance. What did you make of it, Harry?'

'Just an ordinary, plain pot,' said Harry. 'Nothing special. I can put it back together again but, really, it's no great loss. I can keep the pieces for you, if you like.'

The professor nodded. 'Yes, do that, Harry. We've been finding out a few things about the man whose grave it was. He appears to have been some kind of priest or medicine-man. It seems a bit odd that his grave was so hidden. I wonder why?'

* * *

On his way home, Harry forgot about the clay whistle in his pocket. He stopped for a coffee in a noisy shopping centre. As he searched his pockets for money, he felt the whistle in his pocket. When he had sat at his table he took it out to look at. It was still dirty. He gently cleared away the dirt. There was something written on the whistle. The marks looked like writing. He looked more closely and recognised some old Chinese writing. There was very little of it. All it said was: BE STILL.

Be still? How extraordinary. What did it mean? He looked at the whistle again. It was the kind that one blew from the top, like a football whistle. He wondered if it would still work. The thought came into his mind that he wanted to blow it. He wanted to very much. The whistle had not been blown since it had been placed in the pot all those years before. He would blow it. It was small – it would not make much noise. Nobody would notice. So he put it to his mouth and blew.

To his surprise, the whistle gave a thin, clear note that was louder than he expected.

Then there was silence. Complete silence.

Harry noticed something else, too. Everything was still. Nothing was moving. No noise, no movement.

Nothing.

People who had been walking were frozen in mid-step, like statues. They were as still as photographs.

But they weren't photographs. They were real people. Frozen people. Harry's eyes opened wide with surprise. He couldn't believe it. This should not be happening.

But it was. He looked around and saw frozen smiles, frozen steps, a fly frozen in flight, a ball thrown by a child which lay frozen above the hand which was waiting to catch it.

And all the while a total, perfect silence.

Harry sat down again. He could hardly think. How could he make sense of this? This had happened after he had blown the whistle. Had the whistle done this? What would happen if he blew it again? He certainly didn't want things to remain as they were!

He blew the whistle again. Once again it gave its thin, clear note.

All at once the normal world returned. Normal sounds, normal movement. The fly flew, the ball was caught, people laughed and talked.

It was as if nothing had happened.

Harry was shaken. He put the whistle in his pocket. He would have to think about this. He would have to think hard.

But by the time Harry had got home he had somehow persuaded himself that he had imagined everything. He felt better after a good supper and some TV. It had all been a waking dream. He was tired, that's all. He just needed a good night's sleep.

And so he slept. But his sleep was troubled and his dreams were full of shadows.

* * *

Harry went back to work the next day. He found nothing interesting. That's what he told Professor Teo.

'Are you certain, Harry?' asked the professor. 'Whoever buried this man was afraid of him, that's for sure. His body was covered in pieces of paper with words on them. Words which were meant to keep harm away. Strange.'

Harry thought about the whistle. It was still in his pocket.

'I'm certain, Professor,' said Harry. 'I found nothing unusual. Nothing at all.'

* * *

Harry didn't drive. He usually got the bus home but sometimes he liked to walk. That evening he walked. He liked to look at the shops in Orchard Road – one of Singapore's busiest shopping areas. There were antique shops which sold beautiful old pots, maps and other things that his heart was hungry for. But he could not afford them. Not on his salary.

His favourite shop sold the most expensive things. He liked the small, beautifully made figures made from apple-green jade stone. They cost a lot of money but he liked to look. Sometimes he would ask if he could examine a piece, as if he were going to buy one of them. Of course, he never did. But he loved the feel of the costly jade in his hands.

He found himself in the shop again. It was full of the things that he, as an archaeologist, truly cared for. Yet they would be sold to empty-headed tourists who had no idea of their real value or beauty. It wasn't fair.

Without thinking, he took out the whistle and blew it. He hadn't planned to – it just seemed a natural thing to do.

And then there was silence. All was still.

Harry felt afraid but excited. So it had *not* been a dream! It *had* happened!

He saw the shopkeeper standing with his mouth open, looking stupid. A customer was pointing something out, his finger stuck in the air. None of them moved.

Harry decided he would look at some jade while they were all still. He took his favourite piece from the shop – a small jade dragon. It was very old and beautifully made. It was lovely. Why shouldn't he have it?

The thought at first alarmed him. This was not the same as taking things from the university. Nobody even noticed if he took anything there. Here he would be stealing, just like any thief.

He looked around at the frozen world. This was surely meant to be. The whistle had come to *him*. He should use it. Why not? It was only right. It was far better that such beauty should go to him rather than stupid people with more money than sense. It was only fair.

But he would have to do it right. If he was the last one to be seen with the jade dragon he would be looked for once it had gone. He blew the whistle and the world moved again. He waited for a while, then went to the shopkeeper and asked to see it.

'It's a fine piece of work, sir,' the shopkeeper told him. 'And only twenty thousand dollars.'

'It is lovely,' said Harry as he held it in his hands. He wanted it. He would have it. But he made a point of handing it back so that other customers – and the video cameras set up in the shop – could see him do it. 'Thanks for letting me look but I'm afraid that's all I can afford to do just now,' he said to the shopkeeper.

He walked out of the shop, into the shopping centre, out of sight of the shopkeeper. He sat down on a nearby seat, took out the whistle and blew.

The whole shopping centre went still and silent.

Harry felt more excited than he had ever felt in his life. He could walk into any shop he liked and just take whatever he wanted. Anything at all. And nobody would see him. It was perfect.

But, for the time being, he would just take the jade. He walked back into the shop, took the dragon from its place on the shelf, put it into his pocket and walked out of the shop. He went back to his seat and blew the whistle once more. The shopping centre came back to life. Movement and sound returned. He had done it.

And who could blame Harry Chen for the disappearance of the jade? After all, the shopkeeper had seen him leave after he had returned the jade. So had the cameras in the shop. It had been easy.

As he walked home he felt like a god.

* * *

The little jade dragon was the best thing in Harry's collection. He kept all his things in a rosewood box. He would soon need a bigger box.

And, as Harry slept that night, he dreamed that the whole world was still and he was the only moving thing in it. He and the shadows.

* * *

The next day Harry thought that he would see what the whistle could do. He decided to try it out at work. Perhaps on that old fool, Professor Teo. But, whatever he did, he must not draw attention to himself or the whistle. He was sure of that. It was *his* whistle and he did not want to lose it.

Harry was used to asking questions about things. It was what archaeologists did. It was part of the job. He wanted to find out more about the whistle. The first thing he wanted to find out about was this: did the whistle simply stop things moving or did it, in some way, stop time itself?

It was important to know. He didn't want people to notice that they'd lost time. That would be a problem. But if time had stood still there would be no problem. They wouldn't even know about it.

Professor Teo came into Harry's office. This could be his chance to test the whistle.

'Harry,' said the professor. 'I've got some news about our grave.'

'News, professor?' asked Harry.

'Yes,' said the Professor. 'We've been in touch with a local Chinese priest who knows all about this kind of thing. But it wasn't easy. He had to look in the oldest books he could find before he could tell us who this man was. And I was right, it is all rather strange, to say the least.'

Harry felt a sudden coldness run down his back.

'So who was he, Professor?' asked Harry.

'His name,' said the professor, 'was Lou Foo, which means "the tiger". He was a priest who was thrown out by the other priests.'

'Why?' asked Harry.

'The priest who told us this wouldn't say why, exactly,' continued the professor, 'but I think this Lou Foo must have done some very bad things. The priest even warned us to be careful, even though this man has been dead for all these years!' Professor Teo laughed. 'Honestly! You'd think he was going to rise from the dead the way that priest talked about him! Still, it all makes our job that bit more interesting, doesn't it, Harry?'

Normally Harry would have laughed at such things along with the Professor. But his throat felt tight and dry for some reason.

'Er . . . I suppose so, professor,' he answered nervously.

Professor Teo turned to look out of the window, a habit of his. Harry knew that this was his moment to try out the whistle. While the professor wasn't looking, he took out the whistle and blew it.

Then all became still. All became silent.

Harry clapped his hands in front of the professor, shouted at him and waved his hands in front of his face. Professor Teo did nothing. He was like a figure made of stone. Exactly as expected. Harry then waited for exactly five minutes – he counted the seconds himself – before blowing the whistle again. The world of sound and movement returned and the professor turned towards him.

'Is everything all right, professor?' asked Harry.

'Of course, Harry. You know I don't believe any of that kind of rubbish. I'm fine,' the professor told him.

'No,' said Harry. 'I mean, you didn't hear anything just then, did you?'

'Only the birds and the traffic, Harry,' said Professor Teo. 'Was I meant to?'

'No, of course not,' said Harry. 'It must have been my ears making funny sounds. I have a bit of a cold and it gets to my ears as well. Sorry.'

'Well, if you are unwell you must rest, Harry. Take care,' said the professor as he left the room.

Harry quickly went to the telephone to call the speaking clock. When he put the telephone down he knew. No time had passed while the professor had been still. No time –

anywhere. The five minutes he had counted had never happened to anybody but himself. When he blew the whistle he must have been outside time in some way. So the whistle didn't actually stop movement or sound.

It stopped Time itself.

The other priests must have known what this man Lou Foo had discovered. No wonder they threw him out. The way he'd been put in a grave that was more like a prison of stone . . . had he died naturally? Harry didn't care, for now Lou Foo's secret was his!

Harry felt something he had never felt before. He felt powerful. And his heart warmed when he thought of all the things that were now possible for him. He could now use the whistle to get himself money, knowledge – anything in the world that he wanted. For he, Harry Chen, had power over Time itself.

Harry did not use the whistle any more that day. When he got home he rested well. He would need to plan things carefully. Nobody else must know his secret. Harry Chen had been given a great gift and so Harry Chen would use it. Nobody else. It was only fair.

* * *

Harry thought carefully about how best to use the whistle. After all, he couldn't use it to actually see in the future. That was unfortunate. If he knew the names of winning horses or could find out the lucky numbers in the lottery he need never worry about money again. Never mind.

Best to start with small things before trying out his discovery on anything big. That would be best. But what should he do first?

He decided he would look around his favourite shops for all the things he could never afford before but had always wanted. Just the small, beautiful things he had always loved. Things small enough to carry. Then he would steal them.

* * *

It was the evening of the next day. It was dark outside but the shopping centre was brightly lit, as usual. Harry had already had a good look around. He knew what he wanted and had his bag with him, ready to put his 'shopping' in. He had taken the day off work – hadn't Professor Teo himself told him to take some rest? He had earned a break and he was going to make sure he enjoyed it.

Harry decided to have a coffee at his usual café before making a start. After all, he thought, there was no hurry! As he relaxed over his coffee he smiled at the tourists who were at the next table putting more film into their camera. The man looked fat and rich – just the type of tourist he had always disliked. The woman smiled back like the silly, simple thing she was. The fools. What did they know? He could rob them of everything and they wouldn't know it. But that would be a waste of time. He had better things to do. And there was, after all, plenty of time!

Harry finished his coffee and stood up. It was time to begin. He put his hand into his pocket and took out the whistle. He felt like a child at Christmas who was just about to open his presents. Harry Chen's time had come, at last!

He put the whistle to his mouth and blew. But, as he blew, there was a brilliant, blinding light that shot through his eyes. He dropped the whistle in his confusion. The light did not go away.

It took him a few moments before he realised what had happened. He walked away from his table to see the stupid tourist taking a picture of his stupid wife using the flash from his camera – just as he had blown his whistle. The bright flash was frozen in time. That was all. It was just a camera. But he had dropped the whistle.

He had to find it. He began to look around the bright stillness which was all about him. Then he felt something break beneath the weight of his shoe. He looked down. The whistle lay in pieces.

His heart seemed to rise to his mouth as he realised what had happened. And the whistle lay in tiny pieces on the ground. Harry knew, as soon as he saw it, that it was too difficult even for him to repair. He was stuck there.

Harry tried shouting at the still-smiling tourist, at the waitress, at everybody he saw. But it was useless. They could not hear him. They could not see him. He might just as well not be there. He did not know whether time had stopped for the world or just for Harry Chen. And for how long? Would he live there always, with no future and no past? Would he die there?

These thoughts were passing through his mind as he considered the broken remains of the whistle. Only one part could be recognised. It was the part which had on it the words: BE STILL.

He felt afraid. He felt robbed. He felt a cold shadow pass over him. It just wasn't *fair*.